LEADING THOUGHTS

MEDITATIONS
FROM
THE ARIZONA 100

By Jeff Arnold

2024

**To learn more about Jeff Arnold, The Arizona 100,
and *The 100 Companies*, visit:**

https://jeffarnold.com/
https://thearizona100.com/
https://RIGHTSURE.com/

Also by Jeff Arnold:

The Art of the Insurance Deal

How to Beat Your Insurance Company

Moments With Mucka: Business Building Sessions

Money Secrets: A Little Book of Wisdom

Leading Across the Generations: A Guide to Managing and Motivating A Multi-Generational Workforce

CONTENTS

What's This Little Book All About?

This little book in your hands began as a series of short posts published by *The Arizona 100* between 2021-2023.

Each one was intended to share a train of thought, a memorable experience, or spark a conversation — all in 100 words or less.

Soon enough, these modest little blurbs began to amass into a whole collection of meditations and observations.

Fast forward to Christmas 2023, with my eldest son visiting from his home in Poland, and whilst enjoying some conversation over our backyard firepit, the germination of an idea was planted, to begin consolidating, codifying, compiling the short stories into a pocket-sized book.

If you've been willing to take time out of your day and share space in your crowded inbox to read my musings, then why not bring them out into a more tangible, portable form that can travel with you?

In compiling these thoughts, I sometimes dared to go a little over 100 words — not because 100 is too little, but because sometimes thoughts linger on, take new directions, call for revisiting, or find culmination.

I also decided against arranging them in chronological order, because trains of thoughts don't have the strict schedules and stations of commuter trains.

Some thoughts fit and resonate together, others burst in in-between others, while some hang around in the corner, waiting for their time and place.

I hope you'll recognize that this is a book of open-ended thoughts on many different topics, a free space for thinking through all the different things that life, family, business, and society throw at us, to which we are often called to thoughtfully respond.

As my familiar readers know, I'm primarily an ambassador for the wonderfully glorious industry known as insurance and through my firm RIGHTSURE, which is North America's Most Awarded Insurance Firm, we help people with All Things Insurance.

By sharing this book, I hope to show that the insurance industry is not the stereotype held over from a bygone era — one of the salesmen who needs to convince customers that they need to buy one or another policy "just in case."

Rather, the profession of the modern insurance executive is filled with stretching every managerial and leadership skillset you have ever mastered as technology, artificial intelligence, machine learning, and shifting work ethics all converge at once upon the industry.

Without further ado, here are some of the thoughts that my more than 57 years on earth have bestowed upon me to share with you.

— Jeff Arnold

LEADING THOUGHTS

MEDITATIONS
FROM
THE ARIZONA 100

Spreading Goodness

I'll let folks in on a secret: Finding new ways to help others fuels me.

When I started publishing *The Arizona 100*, I was committed to spreading the goodness of the Grand Canyon State and celebrating the greatness of humanity happening within this place we all call home.

When short little posts on a website about Arizona turn into a book like this one, you realize that goodness can easily go beyond borders.

That's why the *Arizona 100* model is universal: whoever you are, wherever you are, whatever it is you do for a living, you can spread goodness in 100 words.

In times when other media spew negativity, 100 words on what is good and dear will do yourself and others much cheer.

100 words — that's a little and a lot that can go far.

"The roots of all goodness lie
in the soil of appreciation
for goodness."

~ Dalai Lama ~

———————

"Never carry failure forward."

~ Denis Waitley ~

———————

Giving Thanks

Too many people talk about "making a fortune" when we should be thinking about "being fortunate."

The other side of business and money that gets overlooked is just how fortunate we are to be able to try out our hands. All the people and experiences and opportunities we encounter are part of our fortunateness — as individuals, as a business, as a community, as a country.

America is a great land of opportunity, one of the few in the world where folks have the ability to make their dreams come true. It's no coincidence that Thanksgiving is one of our unique holidays.

There's a foundation here for those who are driven and unafraid of failure – from the actor trying out for a role they're not fit for, to the entrepreneur raising capital for a product launch that's ultimately unsuccessful.

America does not punish those who fail, it allows them to use each detour as a stepping stone to eventual greatness. I am thankful for that, and hope you are too.

Being an Ambassador
for the Insurance Industry

Think insurance is the least sexy topic imaginable? Among experts, a truth exists: Make it three years, and you'll (likely) never leave.

There's a reason the industry holds onto people for decades: It challenges an individual's leadership skills and knowledge (even math!) in order to understand how legal contracts – and the intricacies of risk transfer, risk retention and risk avoidance – come together.

It's the really cool nuances that captivate my attention. You're going to surrender an inordinate amount of your income to insurance products over your lifetime.

Think all insurance is the same? Nothing could be further from the truth.

All of my books about insurance cover one point or another on the big map of the industry and its role in the world.

"The Single Biggest Mistake Every Purchaser of Insurance Makes is the Assumption that all policies are equal and only differentiated by premium 'Price.'

Caveat Emptor...

Let The Buyer Beware.

In the world of legal contracts (a.k.a. insurance), like everything in life... You get what you pay for.

Buy The Agent, Not The Insurance."

~ Jeff Arnold ~

———————

"Your money needs direction.
If you want more from your money,
you need to tell it what to do
and where to go."

~ Some Really Smart Person ~

———————

Financial Savvy –
The Gift that Keeps on Giving

While data and analytics drive many of my decisions, I have a real passion for transferring knowledge (which is why I give away as many books as I sell!).

The feedback I'm getting on *Money Secrets: A Little Book of Wisdom* has been astounding. It's an easy read full of simple economic principles – something not being taught in schools today – geared toward the next generation.

I recently met a woman who purchased 14 copies as a stocking stuffer for each of her grandchildren. This season, join her in giving the gift of good advice – perfect for friends, family and stockings everywhere.

If there's one thing *Money Secrets* can help you learn, it's this: money will do what you tell it to do, but first you need to learn its language and expand your vocabulary. Anyone can do it — why not start with you?

Creating Opportunities to Build (and Celebrate) Confidence

What qualities are you cultivating in your kids these days? No matter their ages, laying a solid foundation now will help folks (across multiple generations) going forward —from brainstorming projects and collaborating with peers to joining teams and entering the workforce.

Recently, my daughter's attention has been harnessed by all things equestrian – a notoriously time consuming (not to mention expensive!) pastime. She rides three days each week, mucks stalls on Sundays, and thinks about swapping her deep-seated barrel-racing western saddle for one of the English variety so she can explore dressage. Each and every time she learns a new trick on her horse, my daughter is buoyed by confidence.

What a gift it has been to help grow this young female's self-image. I hope she goes forth in the world cognizant of her power and potential – both of which are limitless.

Sometimes, the horizons of the future are already here in our day-to-day passions.

———————

"Don't wait for the right opportunity:
create it."

~ George Bernard Shaw ~

———————

"Every generation has something
to teach other generations, transferring
knowledge isn't just from old to young,
it is a two-way street"

~ Jeff Arnold ~

Learning Happens Across Generations, Too

I have always believed that when the heart is ready, the teacher will come in – a mindset applicable to many arenas, from business and mentoring to sports.

After winning the women's U.S. Open in early September 2023, 19-year-old Coco Gauff told ESPN, "Different generations have pushed me to do well in this one."

This brief, impactful comment was a nod to her father and primary coach Corey (52) – aka "Captain" – and his decision to step back and hire Pere Riba (35) and Brad Gilbert (62) to fine-tune the prodigy's game.

Gauff's heart was clearly ready to learn from another generation. Is yours?

Imperfections Need Not Mean the Death of Effective Leadership

It can be easy to lose sight of the fact that today's most influential leaders are also human — a fact upon which I'm a big fan of shedding more light on. After all, taking our perceived weaknesses and turning them into strengths might be the greatest superpower of all.

I often joke that "Lost in Translation" is gonna be on my tombstone — a fitting epitaph, I've decided, for someone equally fueled by imagination and innovation.

As a highly creative human, I often find myself bursting with a million ideas… All. At. Once. From time to time, things CAN get lost in translation amidst the enthusiasm (something my wife and daughter remind me of often), which presents fertile ground for self-reflection.

Embracing all of my qualities ultimately allows me to see myself more clearly and also allows for continual growth and evolution — a true win-win.

What would your epitaph be?

———————————

"You can choose courage
or you can choose comfort,
but you cannot choose both."

~ Brene Brown ~

———————————

―――――――――

"The ties that bind us are stronger than the occasional stresses that separate us."

~ Colin Powell ~

―――――――――

Creating Ties that Bind Together

Today's workforce includes individuals from a whopping five different generations, which means folks at the helm of these diverse teams – spanning Baby Boomers to Generation Alpha – will inevitably encounter a range of abilities, beliefs, work habits and communication styles.

In the (refreshing) absence of a one-size-fits-all approach, I've got some ideas about understanding and engaging each cohort – one of many topics I explore in my recent book, *Leading Across Generations*.

If I've learned anything over the past three decades, it's that leveraging the strengths and perspectives of each generation is the key to creating more innovative and dynamic teams.

Leading with Intention

With summer vacation in the rear-view mirror, I've been reflecting on the power that recharging my batteries has on creating a positive work environment – for myself and the many teams I lead.

So much of my role these days (no matter where I'm involved) lies in keeping the energy levels high and helping folks maintain focus. From the soccer clubhouse to any of the companies I run, teammates have questions they want answered and problems they need solved.

As for my job? I'm not the chief problem-solver, I'm the chief asker-of-questions – and regular downtime invigorates me to keep thinking this way.

Running around trying to solve problems yields much less than sitting and thinking about the questions being (or not being) asked.

———————

"Get quiet, be still,
silence your cellphone and listen
for a call from the universe."

~ Jeff Arnold ~

———————

Being a Team Leader

Learning to leverage the strengths and perspectives of each generation allows leaders to create more innovative, dynamic, productive, and thriving teams.

Whether you're a seasoned executive, a new manager, or simply trying to navigate the modern workplace, my ninth book, *Leading Across the Generations*, can be a lifeline for navigating difficult conversations (with different generations, no less) with ease.

Why? I'll let you in on the secret: It's based on real experiences, real problems, real people.

The modern workforce is evolving fast, and creating a cohesive whole is more challenging than ever before. This conundrum inspired me to take a lifetime of lessons, learned over 25+ years at the helm of a diverse team, and turn them into a proverbial playbook.

Real leadership calls for being able to field a whole team of different players.

Here's a free copy of my
"Leaders Tip Sheets
for Difficult Conversations":

It's Summertime and the Livin' is (a Bit) Easier than Usual

Periodically recharging my batteries goes hand-in-hand with connecting with family – both of which keep me on track to be a positive human and a good leader.

For much of the year, my wife shows great understanding for my 14-hour-plus work days with a single caveat: Come summer, when she says go – we go.

We are very fortunate to be able to escape the Arizona heat and spend several weeks on the California coast. While my wife needs to be near the water, I simply need to be where I can think – our tried-and-true recipe for compromising and (personal) team building.

You can't think and lead on dead batteries and recharging them requires finding the right port.

Speaking of batteries,
my father-in-law often remarked
that his company's guidance
for success was quite simple:

"Don't sell a battery, solve a problem."

~ Ronald Rezetko ~

Founder, Batteries Plus

"We're living in an era where
capturing moments using
our phones is more important
than actually living these moments
with whomever is beside us."

No Cell Phone for My Daughter... Yet

My wife and I may be luddites, or worse, horrible parents, but we are keenly aware of the unrelenting peer pressure, societal influences, and exponentially increasing youth depression rates that come with smartphones and "social" media.

So we committed to extending our daughter's innocence by delaying her access to a cell phone. My daughter and her older siblings don't agree, as a few hundred eye rolls, foot stomping and protests prove. My wife is stronger than me at enforcing this, and hopefully we are raising more connected, better humans.

Aren't phones supposed to connect us? Instead, they have my family sitting next to each other – yet seemingly miles apart. Even worse, they can disconnect you from real life and plug you in to so many worthless or negative trends, anxieties, and conflicts.

In today's world, you simply NEED a phone to do many things, but isn't it also true that you NEED to set it aside to see what's really needed?

A Love Letter to Arizona

The sun rose over the rugged landscape, casting a warm glow over towering red rocks and sprawling cacti. A lone hawk soared overhead, surveying the vast expanse of desert. A coyote howled, its mournful cry echoing across the valley.

The air was dry and hot yet filled with the sweet scent of blooming wildflowers. As the day unfolded, the sky transformed from a deep blue to fiery orange and pink, a spectacular sunset that seemed to last for hours.

It's in these moments, when nature put on its most stunning show, that the true beauty of Arizona is revealed.

Thank you, Arizona, for hosting myself, my family, my business, and so many unique forms of life and views.

As Arizona testifies, one can thrive in the desert.

Let's take a second to put down our phones and media and look up.

"Then the wind blew cool
through the pinyons on the rim.
There was a sweet tang of cedar
and sage on the air and that indefinable
fragrance peculiar to the canyon country
of Arizona."

~ Zane Grey ~

What Makes America Great

I come from a family of soldiers and preachers. My grandfather, step-father and I were in the Army – my brother still serves.

Candidly, I hadn't been exposed to anti-America sentiment before social media, though I now notice it tends to disappear as folks grow older.

Many of us lament the good old days. Me included. Yet, the America I love is filled with people who believe different than me, worship a different God than me, and have distinctly different viewpoints than me.

I submit to you that, in the end, the variety of viewpoints each of us holds is what makes America so GREAT.

Here's a free copy of my book
The Magic of America,
where I share 76 inspirational quotes
from great American leaders
and writers:

"A man convinced against his will is of the same opinion still."

~ Dale Carnegie ~

To Actually Make America Great Again, Tone Down the Vitriol

If all Americans thought exactly the same way, we'd be a boring country. Fortunately, we don't have that problem – perhaps just the opposite.

It seems that to keep the peace we don't know what to say to each other. I fear we're getting further apart from each other — are we already different countries?

That's the vibe I'm picking up. I hope we can reverse it.

If we truly loved each other and our country, we'd appreciate how others think differently. We'd allow others to have alternative beliefs. We wouldn't be militantly confrontational in expressing our opinions, nor crucify others who differ from us.

Let's find common ground as Americans.

Polar Opposites as Friends

My best friend and I could not be further apart from each other on the topic of religion, but that doesn't separate us. He doesn't believe in celebrating birthdays, yet our family invites him to our birthday celebrations. We're happy to receive him and his family in our home. They don't get upset that we're celebrating a birthday and we don't get upset they don't bring presents or recognize the reason for the event. We love playing golf together and we find plenty of interesting topics to discuss on the course that unite rather than divide us.

Or another example: after speaking at a corporate event about my books, I found a seat at a restaurant counter and struck up a conversation with the man next to me. I live 60 miles from the Mexican border. He lives even closer to Canada's border. We quickly discovered how opposite our views are on immigration. It was a spirited, civil discussion. We parted as friends, agreed to stay connected online and respect our differences.

That's how life used to be in America – and can be again.

"Our differences are our
strength as a species
and as a world community."

~ Nelson Mandela ~

Social Media Made Me "That Guy" – Not Anymore!

I hate to admit it, but I used to be addicted to social media. I'd look at my phone at every red light. I was that guy. One day, I pulled into QuikTrip and before I left the lot, I spent 40 minutes looking at Facebook. I looked in the mirror and said, "I've got a real problem. I'm wasting all my time. I'm an addict. I have a business to run, a family to provide for, children to mentor." I went home and deleted all the social media apps on my phone.

I'm much happier now, and a lot more productive. I realized I hadn't been feeling overworked, just overwhelmed.

What've I done with my new-found time? I've increased affirmation time. I'm more present at mealtime. Instead of screens, I look my family in the eye and ask open-ended questions about their day. I've also realized that the media wasn't informing me, just agitating me. Now, instead of being agitated and absent, I have the time and energy to really be an informed citizen and honest person — by thinking and talking with others. Join me.

"I finally realized it...
people are prisoners of their phones.
That's why they're
called CELL phones!"

"Doing emails often means doing other people's work for them."

~ Jeff Arnold ~

It's Not Only Social Media — Beware of Emails!

Emails are also a problem. And that in and of itself can be an even bigger problem for entrepreneurs and business leaders.

Yes, I'm too easily distracted. But I've got a thousand things to do each week – I'd like to grow my various companies. I want to write more books. I have to look at more financial reports. I need to encourage my excellent team and support more nonprofits.

I've concluded that emails are other people's work. Now, I start my day with my priorities rather than getting sucked into my inbox.

The emails are still there when I'm ready.

Life as a Comedian — Joke's on Me!

In school, I thought I was hilarious. "Oh, Mr. Funny Man," teachers said as they sent me to the principal. For two years after college, I tried being a professional comic. I performed at comedy clubs in California and Arizona.

I've never taken drugs, but I experienced a high whenever I killed it on stage. When I bombed, the lights seemed hotter, my sweat glands went crazy, and I couldn't sleep for a day. It was the lowest low.

On stage I worked with big names. These days, I just torture my family with dad jokes.

Sometimes, one of your skills, hobbies, or unique personality qualities is meant to be just that, not a career. But never discard a part of yourself, especially when you can make yourself and others laugh.

"A person without a sense
of humor is like a wagon
without springs. It's jolted
by every pebble on the road."

~ Henry Ward Beecher ~

―――――――――

"Discipline is not punishment.
Discipline is changing
someone's behavior."

~ Nick Saban ~

―――――――――

Military Discipline —
Just What I Needed to Learn

I was a horrible student. My high school counselor spent 30 minutes with each of my classmates suggesting colleges. He spent three minutes with me and said, "Get a job or join the Army."

At 04:00 am the day after graduation, I was on a bus to basic training. If I stepped out of line, I'd have to run an extra hour. I discovered discipline and exercise. The entire experience shifted my brain.

Finally, I was ready to learn. I spent Saturdays in the library reading everything – Adam Smith, economics, politics, finance, leadership. I couldn't get enough knowledge. I still can't.

The freedom of learning requires the discipline of the learner.

Being a Dad is Wonderful...
and a Work in Progress

Being a father is the most wonderful role with endless trials and tribulations – all of which I wouldn't trade for anything.

Most parents say they love each child the same. My four children each fill a different part of my heart.

Each tests different parts of my parenting skills.

Every child cuts the cord, follows his or her own path and takes a journey that I didn't myself take. It's tough to give counsel when they choose different paths. I don't have all the answers.

The best dad advice I can give other dads is simple: "Love unconditionally."

"Nothing can ever separate
you from my love."

~ God (also, every parent ever) ~

———————

"Parenting is hard,
especially trying to be
patient with little versions
of impatient you."

———————

Being a Better Parent

I've learned that, as a parent, I'm supposed to listen to my children's problems and not do what I'm hard-wired to do — solve them as soon as possible. In my day job, I'm good at solving problems. Outline a complex issue with lots of roadblocks and my mind goes right to work. I'm a solution machine. That doesn't work at home – as a parent or a husband. I have to remind myself to shift gears and be a different person than I am at work.

Listening to my children's issues and silently repeating every word they say centers my mind, forcing me to be present rather than rushing to solve their matrix.

I try to ask open-ended questions. It's hard for me. I don't have the plumbing to merely listen. If I do mentally solve the issue, I don't share it. I return to repeating their words in my mind.

As they grow, their issues scale too. Even small purchases have the ability to affect them calamitously. Yet I try not to react immediately. Listen – repeat – listen.

Being Sued for $1 Billion Makes Everyday Challenges Easier

Entrepreneurs frequently face failure. The occasional successes keep us going.

I thought I was smart 20 years ago selling my first insurance agency to a bank, but when the bank closed in the 2008 banking crisis, I lost my job and my purpose. I mortgaged our house, got a bank loan and bought my agency back.

Two months later, I was sued for $1 billion. A tumultuous and financially ruinous three years later, the frivolous suit was dismissed, yet the everyday stress was debilitating.

Here's what I learned: focus on today and what's important: serving customers, building teams, loving family, and staying positive. That works.

"At some point, everything's going to go south on you...you can either accept that or you can get to work."

~ Mark Watney
(as played by Matt Damon
in "The Martian") ~

One Day I Added Up
My Insurance Bills —
Then I Started a Company

As a young adult, I thought it would be a good idea to look at home expenses. House, car, food, insurance...wait, insurance?!

I added up the monthly payments for insuring our car, home, family and business. I multiplied by 20 years and that nearly equaled...the cost of a new house or a car. I began researching insurance costs and companies. Then I started my own.

I tell people my company, RIGHTSURE, is a technology firm in the insurance space. For starters, we figured out how to close an auto insurance policy over the phone in 90 seconds.

Dealing with insurance can be an art. Some people realize they need to become the artists.

———————————

"Most people never pause to consider how much they are paying for all types of insurance over their lifetime.

Once they do, they quickly learn it's a staggering amount.

That is the moment RIGHTSURE delivers its value."

~ Jeff Arnold ~

———————————

The Biggest Threat Is One Business Leaders Think Least About

Run a business and you learn one thing: If you don't delegate enough to trusted associates, you won't have enough time to perform your most important duty – scanning the horizon for opportunities and threats.

Our most active threat today is the same one most business leaders think the least about: cybersecurity. Cyber attacks are becoming more sophisticated. Businesses and individuals must take proactive measures to protect themselves.

In my book *Cyber Threats Uncovered*, I detail why and how you need a comprehensive action plan for cyberspace. It's much more than strong passwords, software, firewalls, and employee training — cyber insurance can provide financial protection against ransomware attacks and help businesses comply with privacy regulations to avoid hefty fines.

Out of all the books I've written, *Cyber Threats Uncovered* might be the most important, because it tackles the danger too many people don't acknowledge until it's too late.

Here's a free preview:

Tomorrow's Office:
AI and Excellent Humans

I've been spending a lot of time exploring and implementing artificial intelligence (AI) into our office work systems.

I'm amazed at how computers can write press releases, articles, reports – maybe one day this column. I'm impressed how AI can produce photos and videos and sales presentations – even legal documents and computer programming code.

But while AI can assist us in getting work done and making our workforce more efficient, it cannot replace the famously friendly humans in my company's office. Their devotion to clients and finding the lowest insurance rates is aided by AI but will not be replaced by it.

Dealing with AI while cultivating genuine, friendly human relationships is one of the biggest challenges confronting all the generations of the workforce and business today. We need real humans engaging in real thinking to find the best way forward.

―――――――――

"One of the challenges
in the future will be how
do we find meaning in life."

~ Elon Musk ~

―――――――――

"To keep a customer
demands as much skill
as to win one."

Customer-First Thinking
Reaps Rewards

I've never approached business like everyone else.

RIGHTSURE puts the customer experience at the very forefront of how we approach business from the ground up. It's been the key to our success – as our Famously Friendly Humans have been granted the title of North America's Most Awarded Insurance Firm.

Integrating customer service at the core of our day-to-day business is what led RIGHTSURE to become the award-winning venture it is today.

Assuring customer service is the best way to insure customers.

How the Pandemic Changed
Our Business for the Better

Before COVID-19, I was focused on measuring my firm's objectives and KPIs. Three months of WFH changed that.

We're blessed with wonderful mothers who take great care of our customers, but the isolation took a toll on them.

So we launched a weekly moms-only Zoom group in which they didn't regard titles or talk about work. They focused on sharing and lifting each other up.

Returning to our Arizona offices, we've learned it's not all about metrics – we must go deeper, be alongside our teammates, and ensure they're okay.

More than jobs or money, people need to know we care.

"When the culture is right,
the staff will shine."

~ Jeff Arnold ~

―――――――――

"The only thing we have
to fear is fear itself."

~ Franklin D. Roosevelt ~

―――――――――

Effective Leaders Face Uncomfortable Situations

It's too easy for organizational leaders to focus on their computer, inbox or calendar. An effective leader must leave this comfortable confine and walk directly into uncomfortable situations.

Recently, I engaged employees unhappy with one of my decisions. "There are no emotionally neutral leadership decisions," I confided. "If the decisions were easy, they'd have been made well before they arrived at my desk. By their very nature, half the employees will not favor my decisions because they disrupt their normal workflow and comfort zone. People will react emotionally."

The best leaders are tried, refined – and eventually rewarded – through facing the fire.

Look Beyond the Playing Field

Athletes perform best when they finally "see the field." Attending my daughter's soccer game, I looked beyond the field, seeing a homeless camp at the park's edge.

I wandered over at halftime and met Scott, who – save for a few unlucky breaks – might have been on our sidelines with us. Instead, he was living under a tree, barely surviving. Each week now, my wife fills containers with homemade chicken soup and I take it and other comfort items to Scott.

Meeting Scott and pondering the thoughts he challenges me with, I realize that the keys to being a leader in business as well as everyday life are the same: looking beyond the field, facing uncomfortable situations, and daring to know other people.

"But do houses
in themselves hold
any guarantee that dwelling
occurs in them?"

~ Martin Heidegger ~

"Most men, even in this comparatively
free country, through mere ignorance
and mistake, are so occupied
with the factitious cares
and superfluously coarse labors
of life that its finer fruits cannot
be plucked by them."

~ Henry David Thoreau ~

Hear the Whispers of the Wealthy

I avoid rich people, but I've spent decades listening to wealthy people.

Rich people are on a mission to spend their money. It's not always pretty. They squander it.

Wealthy people are on a quest to leave something to future generations – just as they may have inherited it from previous ones.

Rich people tell others about their money. Wealthy people tell their money to go and make more money.

When wealthy people talk to people about money, they often whisper.

Want to be Wealthy?
Have a Lot of Interest!

Interest is a fickle thing. It can be your very best friend or your most ardent adversary. The poor pay interest, while the wealthy earn interest.

Interest is either the price you pay for credit you are using or the amount of money you are earning on deposited money.

If you are borrowing, it is prudent to know how the interest will be compounded, and likewise, if you are earning interest, always seek the highest amount with the least risk.

Remember, the goal is to be earning (good) interest, not paying (bad) interest.

———————

"Compound interest
is the eighth wonder of the world.
He who understands it, earns it.
He who doesn't, pays it."

~ Albert Einstein ~

———————

"Good words are worth much,
and cost little."

~ George Herbert ~

100 Words

I got into insurance not only because I wanted a more affordable way for people to protect their lives, but also to find ways to help people live well.

RIGHTSURE is a different kind of insurance agency that represents the interests of policyholders, not insurance companies. We also strive to help people around our community by supporting valuable nonprofits and the good works they do around the state and beyond.

The aspiration of *The Arizona 100* is similar: Not only are there easier ways to spread good news — there are good people who need it. Spreading goodness is good insurance.

About Jeff Arnold

Jeff Arnold is the founder of North America's most awarded insurance firm, RIGHTSURE, and four-time bestselling author. Jeff has been called a Thought Leader and Global Ambassador for the insurance industry. Over more than 30 years in insurance world, Jeff has been involved in over 60 major transactions involving the sale/purchase of agencies, MGA's, and companies. He serves on the editorial team of *The Arizona 100*.

Let's share thoughts together!

Do you need media placement? Do you want to position your Arizona company or client as an industry thought leader? *The Arizona 100* can get you started and keep you in the running! Our award-winning team can:

- Manage your newsletter and website platform in every city and every town in Arizona.

- Handle all the back-end work — content, design, production, distribution, list-building, etc.

- Deliver your thoughts, stories, and business to more than 100,000 readers in the tried-and-proven multimedia forms they love, featuring articles, images, and podcasts.

The secret formula of our years of success can be yours!

Reach out to us at *thearizona100.com*

Made in the USA
Columbia, SC
22 April 2024